what not to wear
for every occasion

Trinny Woodall & Susannah Constantine

what not to wear

for every occasion

Photography by **Robin Matthews**

RIVERHEAD BOOKS
NEW YORK

to Sten and Johnnie for their continued love and support

thanks

Susan and Jinny for their patience, inspiration and faith in us

Michael and Ed who without each other couldn't have us and the book

Charlotte for making the most of an aging situation

Lucy for never saying no

Pookie for taking the concept of work experience to a new level

Zelda and Christiano for combing out our worries and our hair

Robin and Aitkin for making two old hags look vaguely respectable

David for being as wonderfully anal as Trinny

Riverhead Books
Published by The Berkley Publishing Group
A division of Penguin Group (USA) Inc.
375 Hudson Street
New York, New York 10014

WHAT NOT TO WEAR FOR EVERY OCCASION

Copyright © 2003 by Susannah Constantine and Trinny Woodall
Design and layout copyright © Weidenfeld & Nicolson 2003
Cover design copyright © Claire Vaccaro
Photography by Robin Matthews
Hair by Zelda at Richard Ward Hair & Beauty, 162B Sloane St.,
Knightsbridge, London
SW1X 9BS

Makeup by Charlotte Ribeyro
Styling by Lucy Page

Previously published in the UK by Weidenfeld & Nicolson, 2003, by
arrangement with the BBC.
First Riverhead trade paperback edition: May 2004
Riverhead trade paperback ISBN: 1-59448-050-8

This book has been catalogued with the Library of Congress.

Printed in the United States of America

10 9 8 7 6 5 4 3 2 1

contents

In the first **What Not to Wear** book we laid down the rules of how to match the right clothes to **the most common figure faults**. This manipulation of the truth went a long way toward helping wipe out worry spots altogether. You'd think that such a clearly laid out, connect-the-dots approach would leave no room for more words of wisdom. Well, while it goes a long way to eradicating tapered trousers and exposed mounds of mottled arm, there is still a vast area of **"what to wear when"** not catered for. It's all very well having big boobs neatly encased in plummeting necklines and saddlebags disguised to the point of nonexistence, but all this trickery can be utterly obliterated if you are **dressing inappropriately for the occasion**.

Sad though it is, there's no getting away from the fact that, these days, we are **judged by the way we look**. Some strong, secure, independent women say they couldn't care less about the opinions of others, but we know that they're lying through their teeth. Who in her right mind would rather be a wedding-day embarrassment than the star guest in danger of **outshining** the bride? And while you might not admit it, this feat would give you more of a lift than Prozac.

No matter what a woman's age, she is faced with a series of milestones, special events and occasions that all require careful dress planning. In **What Not to Wear for Every Occasion**, we aim to guide the misguided into looking the part for all manner of life-changing moments. The book demonstrates how dressing well can help you get what you want. It will train those bound by what the neighbors say to **break free from stereotypes**. It will urge those who are lacking in confidence to go the extra mile in order to gain that much-needed self-belief to win the job, get the guy, or fit in with the sleek sophisticates oiled up on the beach in southern Spain. It will enable girls to make **dressing decisions on their own**, without the help of competitive peers, and help make dates for the newly single exciting rather than excruciating.

The book appears to be offering **miracles** and in a sense it does. Nearly all women understand the horror of realizing that you're wearing the wrong clothes. We are hard-wired to know that dressing suitably, **yet with individual flair**, will make us feel on top of the world, but so many of us just don't have the wherewithal to get there.

Were you aware that dressing head-to-toe in one designer label, complete with matching bag and shoes, may look coordinated but shows no **imagination** whatsoever? Are you privy to the secrets of not resembling a lobster in a bikini, even if you've burnt like one? Do you know how to win over a prospective boss or make **speedy transformations** from daytime workwear to evening glamour? Do you like being over- or underdressed at a party and are you happy shocking the priest at a church wedding?

The moral here is to consider the **occasion** more than yourself before deciding what look to opt for. If you do this, you're less likely to make a fool of yourself by turning up adorned in full-length mink at the Animal Rights convention. It's **rude and thoughtless** to arrive unkempt and shabby when your hostess has gone to great lengths. Think how upset you'd feel if your marquee was littered with guests wearing sneakers and jeans when you had spent months and thousands creating a wonderland of elegance?

As important as the event is **what you want to achieve at that moment**. Don't be fooled into thinking your knight will want to ravage you when you're cloaked in velour, or an interviewer will be telepathic and see into your genius brain through a barbed armor of missing buttons and slutty shoes. You need to let your true **personality** shine through while respecting the nature of the event and being aware of how others might view you. If, for example, you're a lively, vital type, it's criminal to murder your spirit by over-matching. Uniform dressing is the quickest way to stamp out any individuality, while a little **risk taking** is the fast-track to getting noticed.

The most common dressing dilemmas are demonstrated in the book by showing what Miss and Mrs. Average might wear versus the kind of cool adopted by Miss and Mrs. Individual. On the left-hand pages you will see the most stereotypical fashion "looks," adopted by women who are lost in choked lifestyles and have no time for clothes. Labelled with a big fat X, these outfits are **nondescript and have no impact**. Some of them may seem smart or even rather nice. Well, they could well be . . . for a different occasion, on your mother or in a bygone era.

The collection of outfits assembled on the right-hand pages and, yes, you guessed it, marked with a luscious "check," are there to be used as **yardstick solutions**. If you like the looks and have similar clothes and shapes to us, then go for them. If, however, you think we look like crap, adapt them to your own personality, shape and style. The **tone** of the outfits, rather than their exact composition, is what we hope to help you with. The looks can be varied by the amount of **accessorizing** you apply. Your aim should be to stand out as a chic woman, not look like the notions counter at Woolworths.

Each chapter is defined by an occasion and most are divided into **"Smart, Casual and Trendy"** themes. Unless you are an old trout hankering after teenage years or a filly desperate for some premature sophistication, we assume that younger readers will veer toward the **trendy** looks and older babes will prefer the **smart** ones. Those who know their shape and how best to flatter it will quickly see that all the looks can be adapted to suit **different ages, sizes and budgets**. Casual has a foot in both camps and the outfits are adaptable for any age.

The **"What it says about you"** quote under each picture is like having a neutral friend whispering the truth on what your clothes say about you. It tells you that clothes can be more effective than you might think—in both a **positive and negative** way.

If you think we have turned occasion dressing into a science that needs to be studied for years as a post-graduate course, you couldn't be more wrong. Sure, it takes time to look great, but only from the point of **planning ahead**. If you have the dress, don't leave finding the crucial shoes to the last minute. Look at your clothes and work out which pieces are the **most adaptable** with a change of accessories. The best jacket, for example, is the one the girls envy when you wear it with jeans and a T-shirt, yet pulls blokes when the T-shirt is dropped and the jeans are replaced by a tight pencil skirt. Your core wardrobe should be one that works for your body shape and can be added to and transformed. With this in mind, along with a little inspiration from within these pages, living with clothes can become hassle-free and frivolous.

In **What Not to Wear** we aimed to wipe out the phrase "Does my butt look big in this?" With **What Not to Wear for Every Occasion** we'd love to eradicate the panic of "I've got nothing to wear!" We so empathize with the agony of trying to look your best when the cupboard is bare or your staple seduction dress for some reason doesn't work on a Tuesday. It's Murphy's Law that just when we're most rushed, or in need of looking our most spectacular, our clothes will let us down.

That's when you want your best friend, wardrobe-side, to advise you. But she may not be there when you most need her. She may also want to outdo you that night. We are much more reliable, so think of us as your **best friends** instead. We may only be peering from these pages, but at least our advice is objective, always at hand and a damn sight cheaper than running out to buy a new outfit for every invitation that comes through the mailbox.

The information ahead is essential to those of you who want to **feel better about yourselves**. We know how much looking good can change a woman's whole outlook on life. If you look chic, not corporate, you'll perform better. If you look hip, you'll have more fun, and if you feel sexy you'll be sexier! **So, girls, look fab** and get the man, the job, the promotion. Win the egg-and-spoon race and out-glitz the hostess at her own party! Most of all have a blast.

the interview Going for a job interview, no matter what your age or your know-how, is a terrifying experience. As important as your resumé, if not more so, is your appearance. When you walk through that door, the inquisitionists will be looking out for dirty, bitten nails, polished shoes, stained clothes, a confident smile. They will be impressed by a positive disposition and assured responses to tricky questions. If you look like crap, you'll feel like crap and perform like a sub-being not worthy of breathing, let alone residing at the rarefied desk left vacant by "the marvelous girl we had before." Unfortunately there is no one solution to interview dressing needs. Your age, experience and the job you are after should definitely be reflected in the clothes you wear. A woman going back to work after her kids have flown will probably be more unsure of her talent than a fresh-faced graduate, so she needs to exude a power she may not feel. The student wants to convey enthusiasm mixed with a desire to commit and willingness to learn. Surely this can't be done with clothes? Oh, but it can. Because in the interview room you are what you wear.

the inter view

1

first job

✗ The suit is predictable and lacks flair

Skirt is too short

Shirt is pretty but overpowered by the black

Too much makeup

Hair is too "done"

Enormous bag is out of proportion with the outfit

what it says about you

"I show my legs to distract attention from a lack of gray matter and I'll be late every morning because I take too much time to do my hair. I'm up for a bit of overtime, if you know what I mean, so I know you'll give me the job."

first job

✓ Entire look is clean and crisp

Trouser suit is more individual than a skirt suit

The accessories, though subtle, show flair and add to rather than detract from the feminine cut of the manly pinstripe

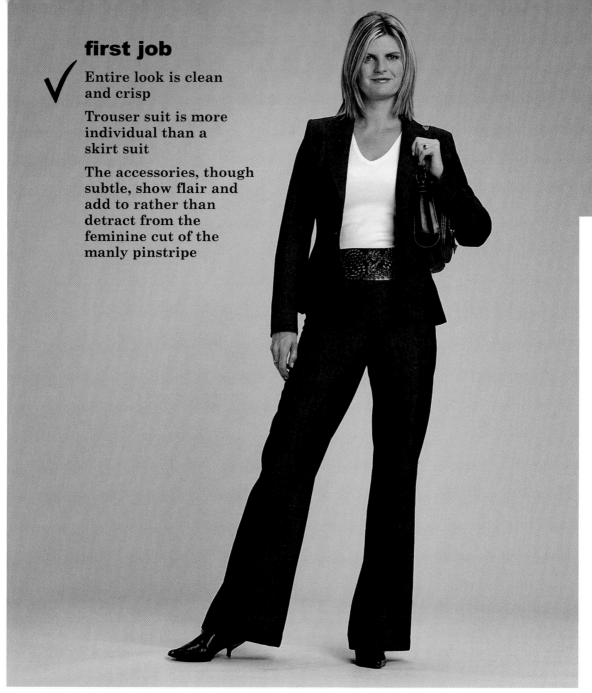

what it says about you

"I don't need fuss or frills because my resumé speaks for itself. Being unthreatening yet confident, I'll fit in with both sexes in the office. You know I'm on the ball because I've got a designer-inspired bag. I like being an individual and I'm ready to take on a challenge."

1

first job

X Combat pants are too scruffy

Tailored denim jacket looks sloppy with the combat pants

Bare midriff not appropriate

Overall look demonstrates a cockiness and lack of personal care

what it says about you

"I'm dressing how I dress every day. I don't think I need to make any changes to the way I look, even for an interview. Take me as I am or not at all."

first job

✓ The coat is a smarter way to wear denim

The trousers are not as casual as the combat pants but still fun

Sneakers take on an air of respectability under longer trousers

what it says about you

"I have respect for myself and this job. I like to be comfortable as well as casually smart–but I won't come to the office looking like a slob."

first job

X So of-the-moment, she can only be a fashion victim

High gold sandals are great for the disco but not the interview room

Everything is too tight so she looks tarty

what it says about you

"I am a fashion sheep who spends all day reading glossy magazines and painting my toenails fuchsia. I'll work hard—when you're watching."

first job

✓ **Dress over trousers looks modern but still smart enough for an interview**

The quirky accessories show personality

Trousers are the right length with the high, strappy shoes

what it says about you

"I'm creative with a sense of fun. I won't be scared to go out on a limb if I need to rise to a challenge in my job. I buy retro clothing to save money, which means I'll be loyal and work hard to get a pay raise."

1

back to work

X **Loose long-line jacket is very dated**

Trendy accessories bear no relation to old-fashioned suit

Never wear matching accessories–shows you were a pushover with the sales assistant, who made you buy the "set"

the interview smart

what it says about you

"I've been out of work for the last ten years, and that was the last time I wore this suit. You may think me dull, but look how on the ball I am with my matching bag and shoes."

1 the interview | 20

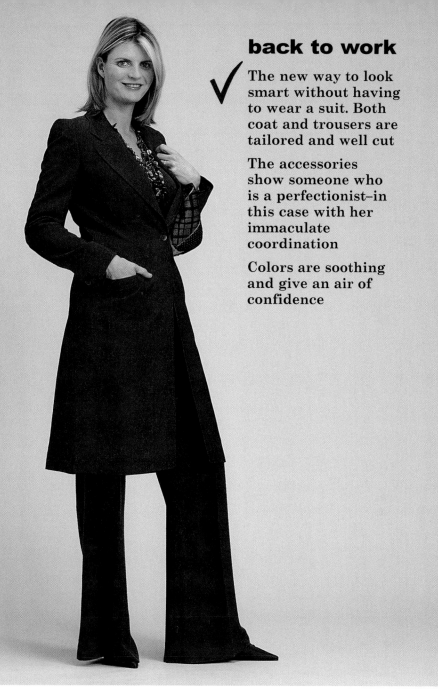

back to work

✓ The new way to look smart without having to wear a suit. Both coat and trousers are tailored and well cut

The accessories show someone who is a perfectionist–in this case with her immaculate coordination

Colors are soothing and give an air of confidence

what it says about you

"Over the last ten years I've taken time out to further my education. I'm very at ease with myself and others, and I'm able to handle any situation. I'm not desperate for work, but I do want to expand my skills."

back to work

✗ Tapered trousers are unflattering and too short for the clumpy boots

Clothes look defensive and as if she wears them every day–no effort made

Shoulder pads show the top to be a good friend from the 80s

the interview casual

what it says about you

"I'm prim and proper but jeez, am I dreary! There's not really much point to me aside from the fact I'll be as reliable and as exciting as the coconut matting on your doorstep."

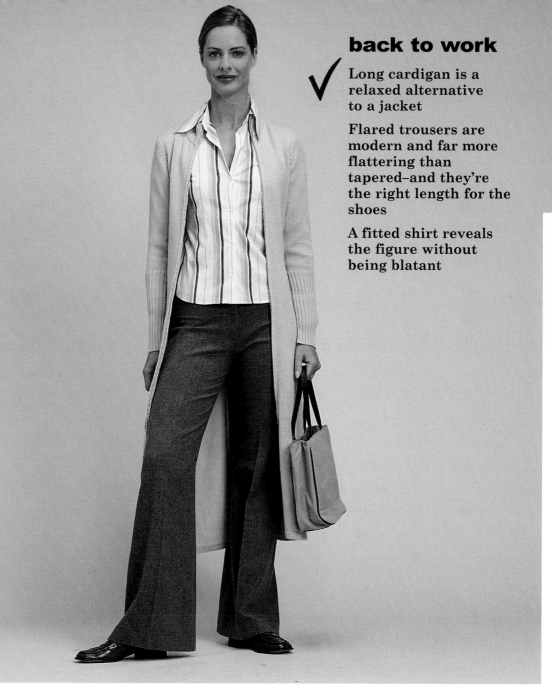

back to work

✓ Long cardigan is a relaxed alternative to a jacket

Flared trousers are modern and far more flattering than tapered–and they're the right length for the shoes

A fitted shirt reveals the figure without being blatant

what it says about you

"It's true, I haven't worked for an age, but it's been great. Now I'm ready to fit in with a team and start a new phase of my life. Clothes aren't the be-all and end-all for me, as I rely on my approachability to make friends."

1

back to work

✗ Everything about this look is stiff

The hair is rigid and was last seen on Flight 001

Scarf is a desperate attempt to jolly up the funereal black

The shoes may be sensible, comfortable and practical, but they make feet look like soup plates

the interview trendy

what it says about you

"I'm terribly efficient and very set in my ways. I don't have a life so I'll never be late–but I will bore the pants off everyone else in the office."

back to work

✓ A dress over trousers is a contemporary look

Muted colors are un-flashy and warm

The bag is fun and a nod to the trend of the moment

Shoes are light and flattering

what it says about you

"I have a natural stylishness, which will be reflected in my work. I'll fit in well with everyone and I have the makings of a future team leader."

the interview/first job

	$	$$	$$$
smart	H & M, Banana Republic, Club Monaco, Anthropologie, Isaac Mizrahi for Target **Accessories** Anthropologie, Nine West, Banana Republic	French Connection, Laundry, Theory, Catherine Malandrino, Joseph, BCBG **Accessories** Furla, DKNY, Hollywood	Prada, Helmut Lang, Gucci, Vivienne Westwood, Chloé, Tuleh, Louis Vuitton, Paul & Joe, Alexander McQueen, Armani, Ralph Lauren, Calvin Klein **Accessories** Hermès, Prada, Tod's
casual	J. Crew, Gap, Zara, Puma, Urban Outfitters **Accessories** Gap, H & M, Claire's	Nuala, Diesel, Miss Sixty, French Connection, Michael Stars, Juicy Couture **Accessories** Nike, Puma, Diesel	Marc Jacobs, Marni, Chloé, Tod's, Prada Sport, Gucci Sport **Accessories** Stella McCartney, Tod's, Marni
trendy	Zara, Gap, H & M, Club Monaco, Urban Outfitters **Accessories** Girlshop, H & M	French Connection, Miss Sixty, Diesel, Velvet, Development **Accessories** Sara James, Hollywood Trading Company, Marc by Marc Jacobs	Marni, Seven for All Mankind, Prada, Miu Miu, Chloé, Etro, Christian Dior **Accessories** Christian Louboutin, Swarovski, Sigerson Morrison, Christian Dior

the interview/back to work

	$	$$	$$$
smart	Zara, Banana Republic, Club Monaco, Macy's, Ann Taylor **Accessories** Claire's, Banana Repbulic, Zara, Nine West	French Connection, Catherine Malandrino, BCBG, Searle, Brooks Brothers, Thomas Pink **Accessories** Anthropologie, Agatha, Charles Jourdan, Kenneth Cole, Joseph	Prada, Chloé, Paul & Joe, Celine, Alexander McQueen, Chanel **Accessories** Celine, Erickson Beamon, Tod's, Hermès, Prada, Sigerson Morrison
casual	Jones NY, Zara, H & M, Gap, Target **Accessories** Express, Gap, Nine West	Agnès b., French Connection, Thomas Pink, Tommy Hilfiger, Polo **Accessories** Furla, Marc by Marc Jacobs, Donald Pliner, Joseph	Nicole Farhi, Prada, Calvin Klein, Armani, Helmut Lang, Ralph Lauren **Accessories** Tod's, Hermès
trendy	Zara, Express, Gap, H & M, Isaac Mizrahi for Target **Accessories** Claire's, Zara, Banana Republic	Nanette Lepore, French Connection, Nuala, DKNY, Catherine Malandrino, Laundry, Marc by Marc Jacobs, Joseph **Accessories** Sara James, Anthropologie	Diane von Furstenberg, Chloé, Marni, Seven for All Mankind, Missoni, Tuleh **Accessories** Erickson Beamon, Me & Ro, Sigerson Morrison

the interview

- Go on the Internet and find out some basic facts about the company. However low- or high-powered the position you're going for, some knowledge shows initiative and interest

- Think of something to ask your interviewer when you're asked if you have any questions

- Take a bath in rosemary oil to wake you up and make you feel more alert

- Make sure you have clean nails and clean shoes, and go easy on the makeup

- Do a stinky breath test with a friend

- Switch off your mobile phone!

- If the interviewer is scary looking, imagine him or her on the loo

- Give a firm handshake and look the interviewer in the eye

tips

1

work wear The workplace is no different from any other environment when it comes to clothes. Even wearing a uniform doesn't give a woman the license to be predictable in how she looks. If you want to stay bland and in the background like an invisible worker bee, fine: stick to corny suits or pleated skirts. If, however, you want to rise through the company, oust the boss, remain in power or catch the eye of the office stud, then what you wear is vital. We aren't suggesting your wardrobe become a theatrical costume drama. Going overboard can be as detrimental as looking the part is beneficial. You need to dress for where you want to get in your job. A uniform of sorts takes away the pain of the morning what-to-wear decision, but it must be made particular to you without offending the boss or causing envy among your colleagues and titters within your workforce. Stylish accessories will set you apart from the crowd and make you feel a little special. This does wonders for your confidence, a feeling that will enhance the way you look and affect everything you do at work.

work
wear

2

the boss

X Hard, severe suit gives an unapproachable feel

Slicked hair with the angular jacket makes for an androgynous look

Skirt length is unflattering for all but the best of legs

what it says about you

"You mess with me and you are O.U.T. I don't like any competition in the boardroom or the bedroom. My career is my life so I only sleep with colleagues."

the boss

✓ Softer lines while still retaining the "boss" image

Kelly bag is an elegant alternative to a briefcase

Stylish, imaginative accessories show a woman who makes time for the finer things in life . . . like shopping

work wear smart

what it says about you

"I'm sympathetic to the needs of my employees, but I still command respect. I have another life beyond the office, which makes me more relaxed at work."

the boss

X The look is sloppy and juvenile

Jeans are fine for casual work but only when worn as tailored trousers

Leave hooded tops at home or give them to your kid sister

Looks like the dog has got at the shoes

what it says about you

"I want to be one of the team and I like my employees to see me as an equal. I do what they do well but do I have the experience and know-how to do more?"

the boss

✓ Even when casually dressed, the boss needs to show authority, which the jacket implies

The flat shoes are good run-around-on-the-feet-all-day type of footwear

Hair is tidy and slick, giving the casual lines of the outfit an air of sophistication

what it says about you

"I'm a doer and happy to pitch in. I'm in touch with my staff, but they all know why I am the boss so they'd never dream of overstepping the mark."

the boss

✗ A plain black suit turns a look into a uniform

There are no details to make the outfit interesting

Nice for a civil service job, but for something more creative? We don't think so

what it says about you

"I'm boring and conservative. God knows how I made it into a hip work environment–let alone got the opportunity to run one."

the boss

✓ Demonstrates style and confidence

Not afraid to wear something a little different and stand out, but because the colors are neutral the look isn't too flashy

Belt shows a good eye for unique details

what it says about you

"I inspire my staff to work hard and I have a strong sense of personal initiative and creativity, which shows in the way I look as well as in what I do."

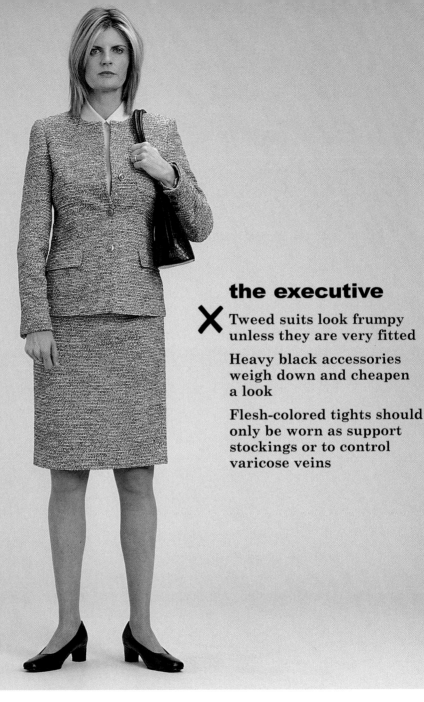

the executive

X Tweed suits look frumpy unless they are very fitted

Heavy black accessories weigh down and cheapen a look

Flesh-colored tights should only be worn as support stockings or to control varicose veins

what it says about you

"I've been in this business for a long time so I know what I'm talking about. That is, until a new client comes up with some innovative ideas that I refuse to listen to."

the executive

✓ Black looks great when worn in softer fabrics

Show off your figure. It will give you confidence

Wear fine fishnets— dead cool with open toes or boots

what it says about you

"I'm smart, sassy and know how to use my sexuality in a professional way to get new business. Looking good helps me to do my job well."

the executive

X Long cardigan worn with the same length skirt shortens the torso

Pale shirt makes features look washed out

Heavy, old-fashioned shoes are highlighted by the skirt length

what it says about you

"I'm old before my time. I've worked myself into the ground and no longer have any enthusiasm for my job, so I'm just going through the motions."

the executive

- Fitted sweater with trousers looks comfortable yet practical

- Wearing the same color top and bottom lengthens the torso

- Trousers are less dated than a skirt

- High heels add a touch of glamour

what it says about you

"Frippery and frills detract from the job ahead, which I take on in a relaxed yet determined fashion."

the executive

X Wearing every trend of the season makes you look like you are obsessed with your appearance

Too much going on here but wearing just one key piece at a time would make it stand out

what it says about you
"I am a sad fashion victim who lives and breathes shopping. The only reason for working is to subsidize my addiction to clothes."

the executive

✓ A velvet skirt can look great during the day if teamed up with chunky leather boots

The nipped-in cut of the shirt shows off the figure

The shirt was bought as a key fashion piece but will become a classic, thanks to its shape

what it says about you

"Those in the know will appreciate my discerning eye for subtler trends. I don't need clothes that do the talking because I am more than capable of doing that myself."

the assistant

X Black and pastels don't do anything for each other

Pale lipstick entirely flattens any complexion

Just because the matching chain necklace and hoop earrings are gold doesn't make them classy or interesting

what it says about you

"I am timid so don't yell at me 'cause I'll cry. I'll arrive at work every day filled with the fear of doing something wrong, so I'll never think for myself."

the assistant

✓ Colors are subtle and work well together

The look is unobtrusive yet individual

The boots add height but don't hinder running around

A fabulous belt is more exciting than lots of gold jewelry

what it says about you

"I have flair, I'm sophisticated and confident. I won't try to overpower my boss, but she'll always be proud of me. When the boss is away, I run the office so well that no one notices she's gone."

the assistant

X Sweatpants are taking the word "casual" too far

No matter how laid-back your job, you should always have clean hair

Zip top looks like weekend gym gear

Overall look says "Sunday"

what it says about you

"I rolled out of bed and came straight into work. I do a lot of office gossiping–and sometimes a little work. I'm a bit of a slacker and my job is not a priority."

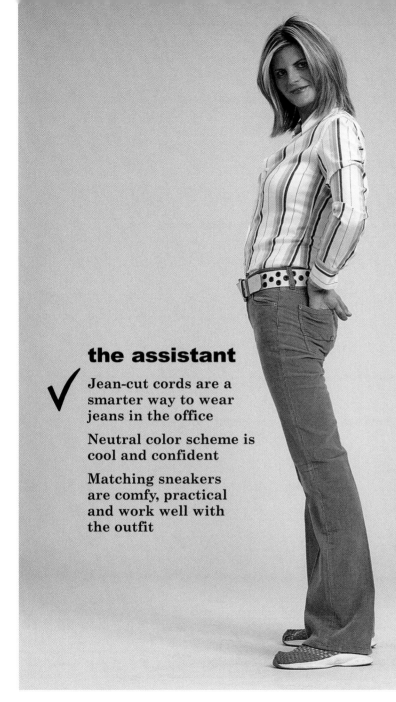

the assistant

✓

Jean-cut cords are a smarter way to wear jeans in the office

Neutral color scheme is cool and confident

Matching sneakers are comfy, practical and work well with the outfit

what it says about you

"I'm a very efficient worker and I'm comfortable in my job. I stay on task, but I also know how to have a good time. Keep me in mind for a promotion and I promise you won't regret it."

the assistant

X

Showing off a bare midriff at work is totally inappropriate

An evening top during the day only works if teamed with flat or chunky shoes

Belt is just overkill

Stilettos are impractical for someone who's running around all day

what it says about you

"I look available and I'll sleep with anyone to try and work my way up. There's certainly no other reason why I should ever be promoted."

the assistant

✓ The skirt is of-the-moment

For height and practicality a wedge shoe works best at work

Looks smart but not like she's trying to outshine her boss

what it says about you

"I'm very aware of everything current. I know how to go far on a tight budget, which is a useful skill in my work. I'm young and energetic and ready for anything you want to throw at me."

work wear/the boss

	$	$$	$$$
smart	Zara, Gap, Banana Republic, J. Crew, Ann Taylor **Accessories** Zara, Express, Banana Republic	Searle, Joseph, Theory, Kors by Michael Kors, DKNY, A. B. S. **Accessories** Anthropologie, BCBG, Agatha, Kenneth Cole	Prada, Hermès, Gucci, Calvin Klein, Balenciago, Chloé, Nicole Farhi, Ralph Lauren, Armani, Helmut Lang, Celine, Michael Kors, Chanel **Accessories** Erickson Beamon, Hermès, Tod's, Balenciago, Chloé
casual	H & M, Zara, Gap, Macy's **Accessories** Zara, Express, H & M	French Connection, Calvin Klein, Nuala, Tommy Hilfiger, Only Hearts **Accessories** Furla, Hogan, Joseph	Ralph Lauren, Plein Sud, Chloé, Paul & Joe, Prada, Gucci, Helmut Lang **Accessories** Hogan, Tod's, Prada
trendy	Zara, Gap, H & M, Express, Isaac Mizrahi for Target **Accessories** Zara, Claire's, Express, Nine West	French Connection, Development, Marc by Marc Jacobs, Betsey Johnson **Accessories** Me & Ro, DKNY, Marc by Marc Jacobs	Jean Paul Gautier, Missoni, Dries van Noten, Marc Jacobs, Comme des Garcons **Accessories** Bulgari, Bottega Veneta, Erickson Beamon, Van Cleef and Arpels

work wear/the executive

	$	$$	$$$
smart	H & M, Club Monaco, Express, J. Crew, Banana Republic **Accessories** Zara, Claire's, Banana Republic	DKNY, Calvin Klein Underwear, Tocca, BCBG, Rebecca Taylor, Jill Stuart **Accessories** Dooney & Burke, Agatha, Anthropologie, BCBG	Vanessa Bruno, Prada, Chloé, Dosa, Diane von Furstenberg, Vivienne Westwood, Nicole Farhi, Calvin Klein, Ralph Lauren, Armani **Accessories** Wolford, Erickson Beamon, Burberry
casual	Zara, H & M, Gap, Petit Bateau **Accessories** H & M, Target, Gap	French Connection, Nuala, John Smedley, Paper Denim & Cloth, Jill Stuart, Joseph **Accessories** Diesel, Puma, Adidas, Joseph	Ralph Lauren, Nicole Farhi, Armani, Chloé, Prada, Calvin Klein, Gucci, Burberry, Chanel **Accessories** Hermès, Prada
trendy	Zara, H & M, Gap Body, Express, Urban Outfitters, Girlshop **Accessories** Zara, Urban Oufitters, Express	Calvin Klein Underwear, Marc by Marc Jacobs, Theory, Joseph, Laundry **Accessories** Sara James, Marc by Marc Jacobs	Prada, Donna Karan, Marc Jacobs, Louis Vuitton, Chloé **Accessories** Prada, Sigerson Morrison, Marc Jacobs

work wear/the assistant

	$	$$	$$$
smart	H & M, Zara, Macy's, Express, Banana Republic, Club Monaco **Accessories** Claire's, Zara, Express, Isaac Mizrahi for Target	French Connection, BCBG, Joseph, DKNY, Cynthia Rowley **Accessories** BCBG, Me & Ro, Kenneth Cole, Joseph	Armani, Prada, Gucci, Dries van Noten, Vivienne Westwood, Ralph Lauren, Calvin Klein, Alexander McQueen, Nicole Farhi **Accessories** Prada, Gucci
casual	H & M, Gap, Target, J.Crew, Petit Bateau **Accessories** Zara, Gap, Claire's	Miss Sixty, French Connection, Michael Stars, Earl Jean, Puma, Joseph, Seven for All Mankind, Juicy Couture, Nuala **Accessories** Nike, Puma	Marc by Marc Jacobs, Calvin Klein, Chloé, Prada Sport **Accessories** Tod's, Hogan, Nuala, Prada Sport
trendy	Urban Outfitters, Zara, H & M, Express **Accessories** Claire's, Urban Outfitters, Express	French Connection, Michael Stars, Marc by Marc Jacobs, Katayone Adeli, Development, White **Accessories** Marc by Marc Jacobs, BCBG, Hollywood Trading Company	Dries van Noten, Marc Jacobs, Miu Miu, Prada, Ralph Lauren, Marni, Missoni **Accessories** Erickson Beamon, Me & Ro, Patch NYC, Pippa Small

tips

work wear

- **Learn to lay out a percentage of your wardrobe by outfits. Makes for stress-free getting ready in the morning–especially if you have thin or fat days**

- **Unless you work at a beauty counter, the workplace is not somewhere to ladle on the makeup–you know who you are**

- **If you work in an office with natural light, do your makeup in the same environment**

- **In case you need high heels for a meeting, keep a pair of simple pumps in your desk drawer to combine comfort with chic**

- **Personal smells can be very off-putting to co-workers and yet their embarrassment might prevent them from commenting. Check your underarms, feet and mouth with a good friend if you're getting dubious looks**

- **Have an emergency kit at work–spare stockings, clean underwear...**

work to play It's always the same. The one night you're going out is the same night your boss asks you to work late. You don't want to let him down, yet there's no way you're going to miss out on the party. You love your job, but not enough to sacrifice your personal life. You know that, but you want to keep your boss believing that you live to work. Keeping this lie alive without having to go to the party looking unwashed and in rags requires cunning planning and an ability to wave a magic wand. It's not a question of having a taxi waiting to whisk you home to a ready-drawn bath and laid-out clothes. That's way too stressful and far too expensive–a fantasy that only happens in fiction. Neither do you want to smuggle in a hanging bagful of glamour that then has to be left filled with the daytime tatters–and probably forgotten–in the party venue cloakroom. Clever transformations happen with the switch of a shoe and the swap of a top. Take heart, dear girls, you can have it all–a successful career and an exciting social life.

work
toplay

3

winter/day

where she's off to after work...

a hot date at a smart dinner party

wants...

to look seductive to wow the hot date, but also maintain sophistication

winter/evening

✓ **how to transform**

Skirt stays, take off white T-shirt to show revealing neckline

Remove coat and show some leg

Change sensible boots for strappy stilettos

Add glam jewelry and fishnets

what it says about you

"I know I'm very sexy but I decide who I'm available to. I am totally in control and any one-night stands or post-coital dumping will be initiated by me."

winter/day

✓ **where she's off to after work...**

drinking with girlfriends – with the presence of some eligible males a possibility

wants...

to look flipping gorgeous – just in case the eligible males do show up – with the illusion that she's made no effort at all

work to play casual

winter/evening

✓ **how to transform**

Un-cuff the jeans

Add a fun sexy belt

Change the thick sweater for a more revealing, fitted top

Add some pointy stiletto ankle-boots

what it says about you

"I'm just one of the girls having fun with my friends, but the one that the boys want to flock to."

winter/day

✓ **where she's off to after work...**

meeting boyfriend's parents for the first time

wants...

to look dressed up but slightly conservative and in something his mum can identify with

winter/evening

✓ **how to transform**

Remove jeans and replace with fishnets

Exchange pumps for stiletto sling-backs

Add an interesting necklace or other piece of jewelry

what it says about you

"I'm a financially independent, well-brought-up girl who only wants to be with your son because I love him. I'm glamorous and fashionable but not tarty, so I won't embarrass you."

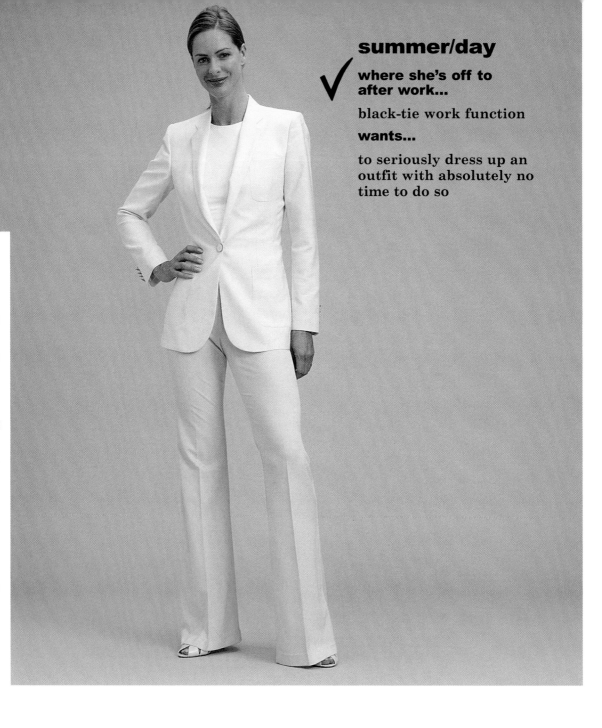

summer/day

✓ **where she's off to after work...**

black-tie work function

wants...

to seriously dress up an outfit with absolutely no time to do so

summer/evening

how to transform

Remove under-top

Put on choker or
opulent earrings

Change to gold
strappy high heels

Let your hair down

what it says about you

"I don't fuss too much with my clothes, I just look this good
naturally. I'm an individual with utterly impeccable taste,
but it's so innate I don't even notice."

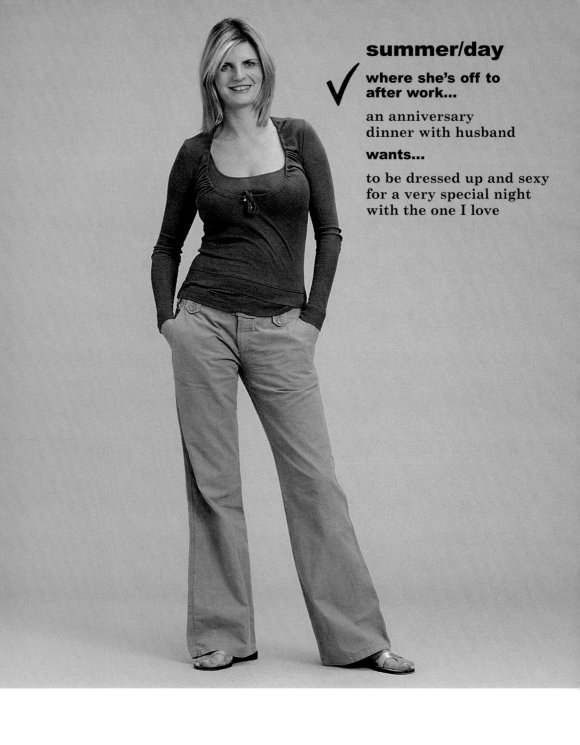

summer/day

✓ **where she's off to after work...**

an anniversary dinner with husband

wants...

to be dressed up and sexy for a very special night with the one I love

summer/evening

how to transform

Swap trousers for long lacy gold skirt

Change bra to one that emphasizes cleavage and makes top look sexier

Add big antique earrings and tuck hair back to show them off

Take off underwear

what it says about you

"I'm your domestic goddess who manages to juggle my job, with kids, home and husband. My sexiness is for you and you alone."

summer/day

✓ **where she's off to after work...**

a summer drinks party

wants...

to crank up the hip voltage in something that's individual and stands out in a crowd

summer/evening

✓ **how to transform**

Switch flats for open-toed high heels

Add extra-long floppy trousers under the dress

Make sure jewels are extra distinctive

Put hair up

what it says about you

"I have a fascinating life. I'm the most interesting person at this party and you can't do better than to talk to me–if I let you."

work to play trendy

work to play/winter

	$	$$	$$$
smart	Gap Body, Macy's, H & M, Zara, Express **Accessories** Claire's, Zara, Nine West, Anthropologie	Fantasie of England, Wolford, French Connection, Calvin Klein Underwear, Development, Diane von Furstenburg **Accessories** Agatha, Sara James, Charles Jourdan, Joseph	Prada, Gucci, La Perla, Chloé, Temperley, Vanessa Bruno, Celine, Michael Kors, Chanel, Alexander McQueen, Givenchy, Boss Woman **Accessories** Pippa Small, Christian Louboutin, Erickson Beamon, Jimmy Choo
casual	Zara, H & M, Gap, Urban Outfitters, Macy's, Express **Accessories** Uncommongoods.com, Claire's, Zara, Girlshop	Michael Stars, French Connection, Anthropologie, Three Dots, Velvet, Juicy Couture, Earl Jean, Joseph **Accessories** Agatha, Diesel, Joseph	Marc Jacobs, Chloé, Temperley **Accessories** Sigerson Morrison
trendy	Urban Outfitters, Club Monaco, Zara, Macy's, H & M **Accessories** Claire's, Zara, Express, Steve Madden	French Connection, Anthropologie, Marc by Marc Jacobs, Juicy Couture, Joseph **Accessories** Agatha, Marc by Marc Jacobs, Joseph	Louis Vuitton, Gucci, Prada, Marc Jacobs **Accessories** Prada, Christian Louboutin, Sigerson Morrison, Jimmy Choo, Manolo Blahnik, Erickson Beamon, Pippa Small

work to play/summer

	$	$$	$$$
smart	Zara, H & M, Gap Body, Banana Republic, Express **Accessories** Zara, Claire's, Uncommongoods.com	Anthropologie, Calvin Klein Underwear, Betsey Johnson, Diane von Furstenberg, DKNY **Accessories** Agatha, Sara James, Kenneth Cole	Chloé, Paul & Joe, Prada, Armani, Calvin Klein, La Perla, Vivienne Westwood **Accessories** Jimmy Choo, Sigerson Morrison, Erickson Beamon, Pippa Small
casual	Zara, H & M, Gap Body, Target **Accessories** Zara, Claire's	French Connection, Diesel, Lacoste, Three Dots, Juicy Couture **Accessories** Diesel, Agatha, Anthropologie	Dosa, Chloé, Temperley, Alberta Ferretti, Marni, Diane von Furstenberg, Dries van Noten, Etro **Accessories** Erickson Beamon, Pippa Small, Sigerson Morrison, Chloé
trendy	Zara, H & M, Club Monaco, Anthropologie, Urban Outfitters **Accessories** Claire's, Urban Outfitters, Target	French Connection, Agatha, Marc by Marc Jacobs, BCBG, Cynthia Rowley **Accessories** Cynthia Rowley, Agatha, BCBG, Joseph	Tuleh, Temperley, Chloé, Missoni, Alberta Ferretti, Donna Karan, Blumarine, Marc Jacobs, Louis Vuitton **Accessories** Pippa Small, Me & Ro, Christian Louboutin, Jimmy Choo, Sigerson Morrison

work to play

- Keep a makeup bag at work that also contains deodorant, toothpaste and cologne

- If you have time, it's better to redo your makeup, especially if you've had a long day and feel tired

- In the summer have some talc and footspray at the office for refreshing sweaty feet at the end of a long day

- Keep a pair of great heels at the office – in the summer, silver or gold and in the winter, black stilettos

- Make sure you have a fresh pair of fishnets in your desk drawer so you can make a quick transformation for a last-minute invitation

- Take out cash at lunchtime – even if you're being taken on a date – so you're always independent

- Have a smaller evening bag handy to take out with you

- Keep vitamin C supplements like Emergen-C in your desk for a perk up before you go out

- If you suspect – or hope – it's going to be a long night and you might have to go straight to the office, have something fresh in your drawer to avoid office gossip

- If your hair is looking lank by the end of the day, slick it back if short, or put up in a ponytail if long

tips

school events There's something about school that makes you feel like a child again. It's the smell of discipline and detention that hangs in the air. Susannah finds herself automatically circumspect in front of her four-year-old son's teacher, even though the girl is a decade and a half younger. She will endeavor to look tidy and together as opposed to displaying the truth of a chaotic start to the day. As a hangover from our own school days, we assume teachers to be disapproving, and as parents we imagine any slip-up from us will lead to the condemnation of our kids. As the children get older, our appearance becomes imperative for the sake of their relationships with friends. If mum looks cool it reflects fantastically on them. If you are aware of this, the pressure of what to wear at school events is high. Not only do you have to score points with the teaching staff, but you also have to win the approval of your children's friends. Turning up straight from being dragged out of domestic mayhem will do neither you nor your kids any favors at all. Combining a nod to what's in fashion with respect for the institutional surroundings will keep everyone happy and your self-respect intact.

school
events

4

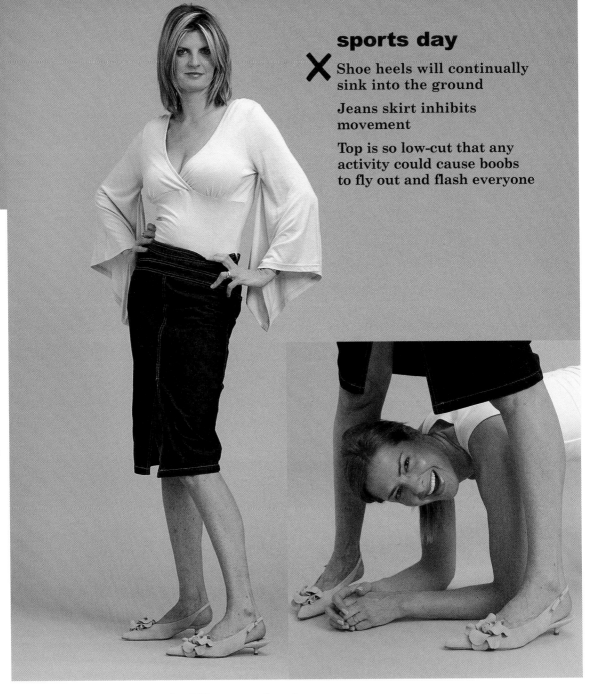

sports day

X Shoe heels will continually sink into the ground

Jeans skirt inhibits movement

Top is so low-cut that any activity could cause boobs to fly out and flash everyone

what it says about you

"I really care what the other mothers (and fathers) think of me and always want to be more trendy and cool than them. Sports day... what sports day?"

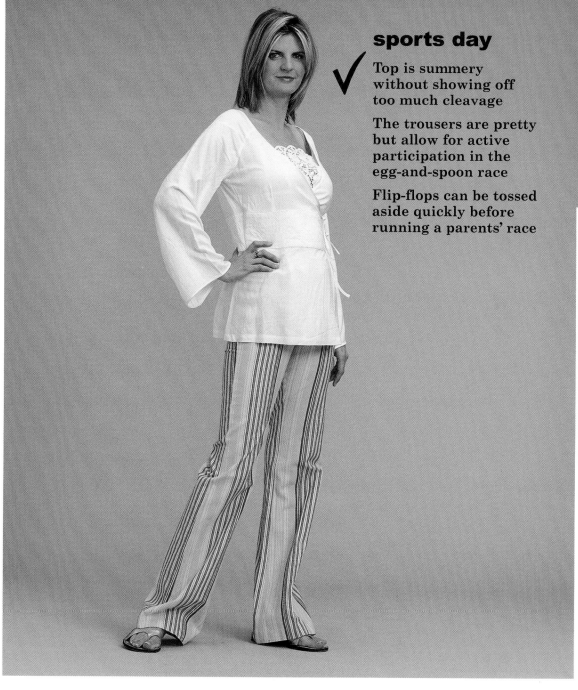

sports day

✓ Top is summery without showing off too much cleavage

The trousers are pretty but allow for active participation in the egg-and-spoon race

Flip-flops can be tossed aside quickly before running a parents' race

what it says about you

"I love sports day and I'll join in and have a laugh. My kids are my focus today but I love to have a chat with the other parents."

school play

✗ Wrap shawls are very headmistressy

Looks like you're about to leave at any moment

The suit and tied-back hair look too stern for a young mom

school events

what it says about you

"My children eat all their greens, say please and thank you, open doors and do their homework on time. They'll go to college and become president."

school play

✓ Similar colors streamline separates

A great coat can change a running around daytime outfit into something more special

Hair down looks more relaxed and less severe

what it says about you

"I am a responsible mother who's sensitive to blending into the audience. I may have a high-powered career but I still make time to look good for my kids."

pta meeting

✗ The jeans are messy and dirty looking

The layered untucked tops suggest a tardy, disorganized mother

Sunglasses on the head remind the teacher of a school rebel who hasn't grown up

Battered shoes look scruffy

what it says about you

"I don't really have time for this because I've got to run to the supermarket. Chaos is the key word for my family's lifestyle. What you tell me will go in one ear and out the other."

pta meeting

✓ Dressing up gets you respect from the teacher

The leather jacket spices up the outfit so as not to look matronly

Layering clothes of the same color adds texture without looking messy

Boots give the outfit a more modern edge

what it says about you

"I respect the school. I'm a responsible mother who's young at heart, and I have enormous fun with my kids. I want the best for them at school and expect you, Teacher, to provide that."

carol concert

X

Red and black bring out the tart in everyone – NOT festive

The combo of a high slit, fishnets and ankle booties smack of trying too hard to be young and sexy

Bright red lipstick is too flashy for the occasion

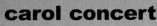
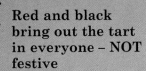

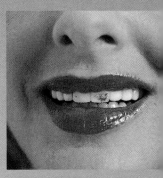

what it says about you

"I am slutty, available and a bad role model for my children. I flirt with all my teenage son's friends – mmm, I think I need a chat with that math teacher."

carol concert

✓ Subtle sparkle is a
merry nod to the
festive season

Dark colors allow
your child, not you,
to shine

Boots tone down the
effect of the sequins

what it says about you

"I'm a desirable Yummy Mummy and my child's friends
will always be welcome and have fun when they come
to play at our house."

school events

	$	$$	$$$
sports day	H & M, Zara, Gap, Target, Urban Outfitters **Accessories** Claire's, H & M, Zara, Target	French Connection, Michael Stars, Calvin Klein Underwear, Three Dots, Juicy Couture, Earl Jean, Nuala **Accessories** Birkenstock, Nike, Puma	Dosa, Marni, Dolce & Gabbana, Prada Sport, Polo Ralph Lauren, Marc Jacobs **Accessories** Sigerson Morrison, Tod's, Prada Sport, Hogan
school play	Zara, Express, Banana Republic, H & M, Anthropologie **Accessories** Zara, H & M, Gap, Nine West, Steve Madden	French Connection, Nicole Miller, BCBG, Michael Stars, Marc by Marc Jacobs, Diane von Furstenberg **Accessories** Nicole Miller, BCBG, Charles Jourdan	Temperley, Prada, Chloé, Marc Jacobs, Vivienne Westwood, Louis Vuitton **Accessories** Prada, Chloé, Jimmy Choo, Christian Louboutin, Louis Vuitton
pta meeting	Zara, H & M, Gap, Banana Republic, J. Crew, Anthropologie **Accessories** Anthropologie, Nine West, Claire's, Banana Republic	French Connection, BCBG, Michael Stars, Nicole Miller, Catherine Malandrino **Accessories** Nicole Miller, Marc by Marc Jacobs, BCBG Kenneth Cole	Gucci, Prada, Alexander McQueen, Chloé, Dries van Noten, Vivienne Westwood, Vanessa Bruno **Accessories** Prada, Gucci, Sigerson Morrison
carol concert	Zara, H & M, Banana Republic, Anthropologie, J. Crew, Express **Accessories** Nine West, Zara, H & M, Steve Madden	French Connection, Nicole Miller, BCBG, Theory, Catherine Malandrino **Accessories** Nicole Miller, Charles Jourdan, BCBG, Agatha	Nicole Farhi, Temperley, Ralph Lauren, Prada, Alexander McQueen, Chloé, Boss Woman, Armani, Gucci **Accessories** Prada, Hermès, Louis Vuitton, Sigerson Morrison

where to shop

school events

- Remember you're no longer in school – so enjoy yourself

- Look clean and tidy but don't overdress or look overtly sexy

- Keep makeup subtle

- If you're not a parent, there are fewer constraints about how eccentric you can look

- Don't overdo the sucking up to teachers. They will only smell a rat

- Too much boasting about your child alienates other parents

- Keep camera paraphernalia to a minimum

- If you have teenagers, don't try to chat too much to their friends and compete with their put-on coolness. You'll only embarrass your own child

tips

summer wedding Ah, the joys of a summer wedding. Balmy air dotted with fireflies; the gentle evening light softening out the skin tone as effectively as Botox; barefoot bridesmaids, glowing from the warm afternoon sun, fluttering around the wedding cake. You cast your eye fondly across the idyllic scene when, all of a sudden, hell arrives in clumpy black shoes and a crochet shawl. It was too perfect to be true, and there's always one guest who lands like a sick joke, fresh from the planet of Bad Taste. The unknown being is confused about the seasons. She knows not if it is summer or winter. Her time clock, too, has gone awry. Is it day or night? Eradicating any chance of catching a chill, breaking out into a sweat or getting surprised by her period, she wears thick flesh-colored tights bulging over wide-strapped black sandals. Her "handy" shawl is easy to discard after a strenuous bop around her giant handbag, which hides a cash-and-carry sized pack of panty liners. She has thought of everything – and it shows in her outfit. She doesn't look chic. She is a one-woman band of fashion blunders. Do you know this woman? If so read on.

summer wedding

5

day

✗ Everything is matching even the bag and hat

Jacket length is dated and disproportionate on any body shape

The entire outfit shows a lack of individuality

If it's sunny, the fabric will be suffocating

what it says about you

"I have no imagination, but I don't need one because all that matters is that I fit in with all the other middle-aged prudes. You know I've worn this suit many times before – it's my wedding suit."

day

✓ A floaty summer dress that flatters the body shape is the most elegant attire for a daytime summer wedding

Look is unfussy yet feminine

Hat picks out the palest color in the dress, not the darkest

Accessories stand out for the key pieces they are

what it says about you

"I don't want to outshine the bride or her mother. I appreciate what a special day it is and have gone the extra mile with my look."

day

X The jean jacket is totally inappropriate for a wedding and shows a lack of respect for the importance of the day

Linen skirt will crease badly during the ceremony

Bag is overwhelming and gives a cluttered look

What *is* that on her head?

what it says about you

"I don't care that I'm still on the shelf and I don't like weddings so don't want to make any effort. In fact, I'm too cool to conform to tradition."

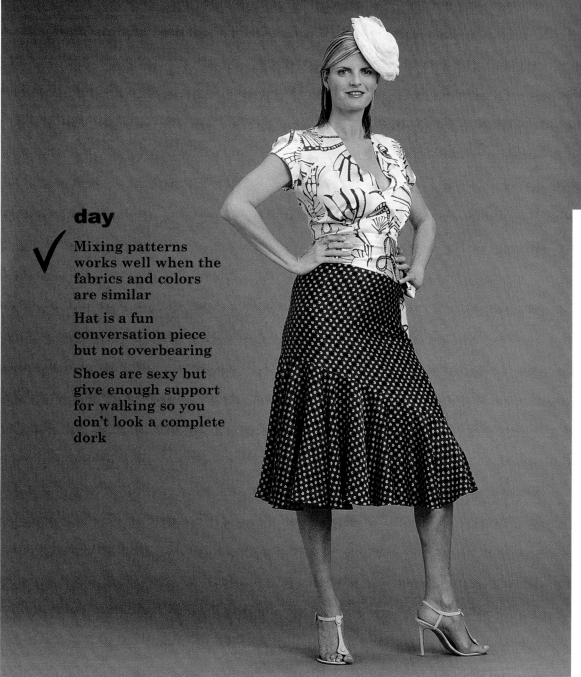

day

✓ Mixing patterns works well when the fabrics and colors are similar

Hat is a fun conversation piece but not overbearing

Shoes are sexy but give enough support for walking so you don't look a complete dork

what it says about you

"I'm going to have a ball. I'm fantastic fun to hang with and I'll drink you under the table but still be together enough to catch the bride's bouquet."

evening

X The tweed jacket is behind the times and too uncomfortable to dance in

Black accessories are too strong a contrast with the pastel colors

The choker labels the wearer

what it says about you
"Once I've got you, you won't escape. I'll go on and on about fascinating subjects such as the weather, my Jack Russell and how I've known the bride since she was that high."

evening

✓ The colors of the outfit echo those in the hairpiece and so bring harmony

A sexy dress to dance in

Slinky cardigan and fab evening bag complete a stunning look

what it says about you

"I understand the sobriety of a religious ceremony, but I fully intend on letting my hair down later when the dancing starts."

evening

X Navy and red never look good together unless another color is involved

The flowers would look better if they were just in the hair

Crocheted cardigans look tired and frumpy

what it says about you

"I need frivolous clothes to compensate for my lack of personality. I'll be hard work to talk to until a couple of bottles have slipped down my throat. Then I'll embarrass myself on the dance floor before rushing off to vomit in the ice bucket."

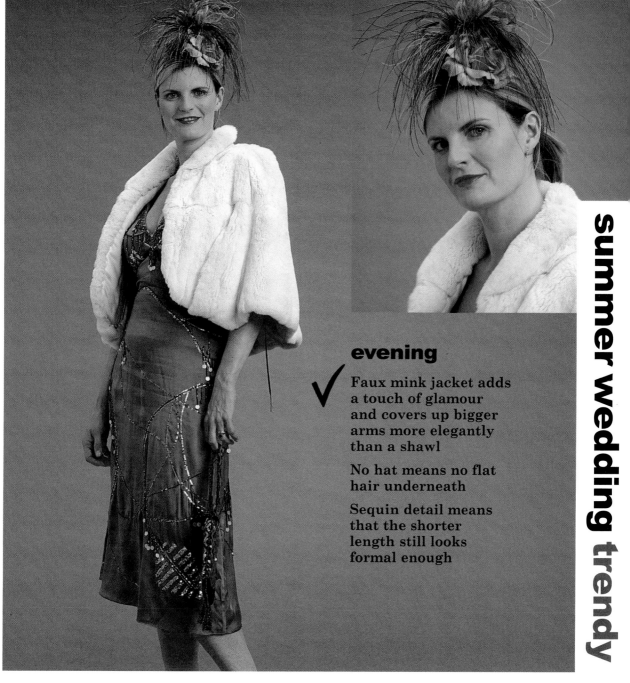

evening

✓

Faux mink jacket adds a touch of glamour and covers up bigger arms more elegantly than a shawl

No hat means no flat hair underneath

Sequin detail means that the shorter length still looks formal enough

what it says about you

"I'll be more than happy to let you peer down my cleavage just so long as you keep your hands to yourself. Once you've met me you won't want to leave my side."

summer wedding/day

	$	$$	$$$
smart	Zara, Banana Republic, Club Monaco, H & M **Accessories** Claire's, H & M, Banana Republic	Anthropologie, BCBG, Laundry, Cynthia Rowley, Nicole Miller, Tocca **Accessories** Agatha, BCBG, Charles Jourdan	Prada, Alberta Ferretti, Temperley, Paul Smith, Chanel, Diane von Furstenberg **Accessories** Jimmy Choo, Manolo Blahnik, Christian Louboutin, Sigerson Morrison, Paul Smith, Erickson Beamon, Solange Azagury-Partridge
trendy	Zara, Banana Republic, H & M, Macy's, Urban Outfitters, Express **Accessories** Claire's, Macy's, Express	French Connection, Nicole Miller, BCBG, Catherine Malandrino, Joseph, A. B. S. **Accessories** BCBG, Marc by Marc Jacobs	Temperley, Paul Smith, Moschino, Marc Jacobs, Jamin Puech **Accessories** Christian Louboutin, Jamin Puech, Manolo Blahnik, Paul Smith

summer wedding/evening

	$	$$	$$$
smart	Zara, Express, J. Crew, Macy's **Accessories** Zara, Claire's, Express	Nicole Miller, French Connection, BCBG, Anthropologie, Marc by Marc Jacobs **Accessories** Agatha, BCBG, Hollywould	Valentino, Prada, Celine, Armani, Christian Dior, Yves Saint Laurent, Alberta Ferretti **Accessories** Swarovski, Erickson Beamon, Pippa Small, Jimmy Choo, Manolo Blahnik
trendy	Zara, Club Monaco, H & M, Express **Accessories** Claire's, Club Monaco, H & M	French Connection, Nicole Miller, BCBG, Diane von Furstenberg, Betsey Johnson, Cynthia Rowley **Accessories** Nicole Miller, Agatha, BCBG	Emanuel Ungaro, Temperley, Chloé, Moschino, Dolce & Gabbana, Tuleh **Accessories** Jamin Puech, Jimmy Choo, Manolo Blahnik, Cartier

summer wedding

- Never outshine the bride unless she's marrying your ex-lover
- If you don't know how to deal with an ex or unwanted attention, wear a wide-brimmed hat to avoid too much physical contact
- Don't wear white at a conventional wedding
- If the reception is anywhere near a lawn, don't wear a thin heel
- Don't carry a big bag
- Trousers are fine – as long as they're not the ones you might wear to the office
- If the wedding is in daylight, do your makeup in daylight
- Get a pedicure if you are wearing open-toed sandals and pay special attention to your heels
- A fan can keep you cool in church and act as a flirtatious accessory
- If it's wet, don't wear open-toed sandals or suede shoes

tips

winter wedding Phlumph! Wedding invitation lands on door mat. "Oh, so and so is getting married. Must get my suit out. Better get my coat dry-cleaned as it's bound to be cold. Thank goodness I bought that hat for Jane's wedding in the summer. It will go perfectly with my bag and shoe set." Do we feel a uniform appearing? For some reason winter weddings are more inclined to bring out the chain-store manageress in women. Sensible suits are much in evidence, often coupled with a heavy winter coat and a navy or black hat that bears no relation to the rest of the outfit. Color is often abandoned in the colder months, leaving a ceremony more in tune with that for a passing relative. One guest might break the drab ranks, but rest assured she'll do so in bottle green or maroon. If there's an evening do, then style spirals into strappy dresses compromised by something warm, as inappropriate as the presence of the groom's ex-wife. While this is, of course, a wild generalization, many of you will secretly recognize elements of the Archetypal Winter Wedding Attire. Relieve yourself from the chains of mediocrity by being an outstandingly stunning guest.